salmonpoetry

Motherlung

LISA MARIE BRODSKY

salmonpoetry

Published in 2014 by
Salmon Poetry
Cliffs of Moher, County Clare, Ireland
Website: www.salmonpoetry.com
Email: info@salmonpoetry.com

ISBN 978-1-908836-89-2

COVER IMAGE: © Bunyos | Dreamstime.com
COVER DESIGN & TYPESETTING: *Siobhán Hutson*
Printed in Ireland by Sprint Print

For my mother, Sheila Brodsky,
my best teacher of gratitude, grace, and love

"and you begin to accept defeats
with your head up and your eyes open
with the grace of a woman, not the grief of a child."
~ from *"A Few Words of Caring . . ."* (anonymous)

A PLAQUE MY MOTHER HAD ON HER DRESSER WHEN I WAS A CHILD

Acknowledgments

Grateful acknowledgment is given to the editors of the following publications in which these poems listed first appeared, some in slightly different versions:

The Albatross: "The Operation"
Boiling River Review: "Can't Stop What's On Its Way"
Loch Raven Review: "10 and 5," and "The Mother Who Wasn't"
Sol Magazine: "Attic Illness" and "Floweret" (published as "The Art of Drying Roses")
Sun-Optikos: "Floweret" (published as "The Art of Drying Roses")
"Suspicion" on *madpoetry.org*

A special thank you to my husband, Lee Auter, and my three stepchildren, Aislyn, Gabrielle, and Atrus. You are the best poems of my life. Thank you to my surrogate mothers throughout the years: Vivian Vahlberg, Audrey Rooney, Mary Rotter Fullerton, Christy Coffey, and Nancy Broberg. Your emotional and spiritual guidance has been pivotal in shaping my healing journey. Thank you for still taking the phone calls.

Thank you to UW-Madison and the Madison poetry community that embraced my wanderings for more than a decade.

To all the high school "kids" who called my mom their mom: Megan Tucker Mueller, Sheryn Novak Panfil, Joseph Monroe, Peter Goss, Franco LaMarca, Rich Russo, Joel Oritz, Suzanne Optie Johnson, and many more I know I am forgetting. I hope her loving memory is lasting in your hearts.

Thank you to my variety of sisters: Lauren DeLegge, Elizabeth Kalk, and Jenny Miller for walking with me during some of the hardest times.

Thank you to my father, Michael, and stepmother, Linda Brodsky, for teaching me love between husband and wife since I was eleven. And for Linda, who always loved me as her own and whose role I now more fully admire and appreciate.

Lastly, thank you to Jesus, who came and swept me off my feet just in time, who taught me that only He should be my Everything and what an Everything. The story of my mom, our love, our pain, this book, is really God's story.

Contents

Part Three: *Griefship*

Part Four: *Stepship*

PART ONE
Mothership

Poem for Sheila Rae Brodsky

after the poet, Jan Heller Levi

Who is this Sheila Rae Brodsky
b. 1954
d. 2006
with her New Year's napkin from every year's bar,
      highlighted moments scribbled down?

Did she have two lives to live?

The first — mother to a beautiful wish put to flesh
who napped with her on summer afternoons
in the little house on Carmen Avenue

The second — years and a lifetime later,
wife to the tall, mustached policeman
who taught her to shoot a gun
and, after the attack, walk tall under
wide open, Wisconsin skies

Here's to her sleep
as we paste our memories on
kindergarten
construction paper
to make it real
to make us feel better about
the life we now must live.

Here's to her hair growing out
so she can suck the tips
like she did as a child.
Here's to her hair growing lush and thick
so we can pack away the head scarves
and finally bury
what ought to be buried.

First Memory

Cradled on my mother's lap
in a rocking chair
with my head against
her vibrating chest as she
sings:
        "The hills are alive
                with the sound of music…"

Ear tickled from breath
smoky-sweet

Eyes blinking tired as I nestle
into her cream, crocheted sweater

        "and I'll sing
            once more."

The Lists I Kept as a Child

are on my refrigerator.
I can't keep the monsters out.
Some slide between
the panels of fence;
some hang
overtop
like ivy.

Some sit at the table
with my mom and watch
me write lists of what frightens me.
She reminds me to be wary
when I walk down the block

because bodies crouch in bushes;
their dog-breath
hangs over my shoulder.

Earwigs dip
and plunge
through dirt,
so fluid
they could weave through hair
unnoticed.
Cicadas circle with
blinking wings.
Alligators. Komodo Dragons.

There are other creatures –
some like rancid jelly
that drip and ooze.

I lose count of how many
there are; this fence
is no barrier.
Each night I recite the list:

Boogie man.
Great White Shark.
Men who raped my mother.

Suburban Sunshine (and Her Shadow)

It's my childhood summer
and Mom roasts under the sun
in her reclining plastic lounger.
She browses *Ladies' Home Journal*
and warmed eyelids close to sleep.

"Get out more," she tells me
in my awkward, pre-teen years.
"The sun needs to see your face."

But I stay inside with my
soap operas and Doritos.

She re-emerges with sleek,
dark tan lines wrapped around shoulders
and sets herself up at the Formica kitchen table.

Her summer snack is a plate of
bread-and-butter pickles, cheese squares,
and crackers.
She sing-songs from the kitchen:
"You should go outsiiiide…"

I stare at Frisco kissing Felicia on channel 7.

The sun is not my friend
as it is hers.
I ache to sail my ten-speed down
blocks of suburban streets,
walk to the pool as I once did,
but the sun now betrays me.

Mom doesn't have burgeoning breasts
or swatches of skin

swinging from thighs.
Somehow, she resembles
a slightly older sister
rather than a mid-30s mother.

She sparkles youth and
suburban sunshine.
I have no desire
to be illuminated.
I stay in the shade of a notebook,
my pen trying to outrun
the weight my body collects.

Legacy

We daughters never learned to weep.
It was up to the mothers
to create a space
where, as babies, we could
let out our frustration.

Where, as children, we
could test boundaries
and cry at our failures.

Where, as teenagers, we
could love, lose,
and cry at our own wanderings
yet return home to safety.

If we did not see our mothers cry
it would feel alien.
If we saw them cry too much -
a threat.

Mothers throw their hands
up in the air; any which way
they lose.

I taught myself to weep;
I believe I was born with the knowledge.
Mother listened to my sobs
from behind a closed door for years.

That's when tears bring on the fear
of continuation
and mothers wonder if crying
should be taught at all
just to save their daughters
from such pain.

When Her Stomach Growled for Me

"When I think of people who kill and eat people,
I think of how lonely my mother was."
~SHARON OLDS, "Freezer"

In the years when I plagued her sanity
she stood on the other side of my door
and knocked, shouted,
begged to be let in.

She knew who I was:
sixteen-year-old using
a stolen knife to test
strength against my arm.

I was angry at her absence
in the story of my life.
Off to work, on a date…
then angry at the paradox of
a sudden hunger for me.

She missed my crawling
into her bony lap,
the both of us cradling each other
in the yellow corduroy chair.
I tried telling her of my day;

back then, I followed her
like she was the sun
and I in orbit,
but she always had
somewhere to be,
her heels pulling
her out the door like taffy.

Then she wanted to taste what I tasted:
cast lists, a boy's note snuck into my bag,
journals asking existential questions
that scattered in the air, unanswered,
like mute sparrows.

Knock-knock. She began to yell,
her stomach rumbling for news
of my dangerous emo condition.
I kept my door closed, kept her starving
just to teach her that you can't
always get what you want when you want it,
whenever the great taste for daughter strikes.

But I admit now: while she hungered for me,
I ignored my hunger for her
and we both grew thin many years hence.

The Mother Inside the Daughter

I was a new three-year-old
when her rape happened.

Listen to that — *happened* —
as though she happened to be late
for the bus.

Happening can mean tragedy to come.

That night in '81 she happened to leave
the kitchen window open
and I happened to wake up
in the middle it all.

She shushed and hushed me,
tucked me back into bed
and returned to her room
in nothing but a sheet.

That night would happen
to become
her permanent wound.

When pieces of us get taken away
we struggle to put other pieces
back together.
I was an overwhelming piece
and knew it.

As years passed
and her senses returned
I helped her stand up, learn to walk,
say the word "trust" again.
I raised her as she raised me.

I lived her fear as she lived
her own, her trepidations,
her protectiveness.

Some would go so far as to say
that, in my twenties,
they couldn't tell the daughter
from the mother. One had swallowed
the other.

Can't Stop What's On Its Way

This is not to say
I have not hated her.
She scrubbed my five-year-old face
as my body fought her clutch.
I cursed her in my teens, when pen and paper
were my only comrades.
Phones slammed down so hard in my twenties
that receivers cried out from the sting.

January of '06: she calmly says they found
a mass on her lung.
We go to brunch, surreal to gather
Eggs Benedict and slices of cantaloupe onto our plates.
It's only while I drink my orange juice
that she says the word "cancer"
and everything sours.

The singe of cigarettes, clear plastic
tail of the wrapper lies on her kitchen table.
She has not quit.
Gramma's pink alligator-skin case still sits
on Mom's bedside.

Perhaps it's not hate I feel just then,
though she shrugs when I ask, "why?"
It's that shrug, that helplessness I hate —
such ignorance keeps her car driving
toward the broken bridge,
blazing bodies lying haphazardly
at the bottom of the cliff.

Cancer's Little Deaths

She lost her job when I was eleven
and I remember her throwing up from drink
and then staring out the morning window
at the busy birds,
cold coffee cup in hand.
She wanted to die then, no doubt,
but I'd come to her for help with homework
or ask her to make meatloaf
and she'd have to get up
and claim her life.

Perhaps she wanted little deaths
to bring her relief.

I understand.

Now she tells me at least cancer isn't
as bad as getting killed by a bus:
now you have time.

I'd prefer neither. In fact, I hated
her metaphors, but perhaps that's
how she coped with each finale of
hair, balance, speech.

Maybe she's more of a poet than I,
her mind whirling in scenarios and images.
I want to live in a world where my mother
doesn't think about death.
Where she wants to live in a world
of two healthy lungs,
a 9 to 5 job
and scotch at bedtime – on the rocks.

Rock-a-Bye

As a baby, I once fell asleep
with both eyes open.
Mom checked on me and screamed,
my seemingly-dead pupils
staring ahead with
black olive detachment.
She shook my belly
until I blinked and fitfully rose
out of sleep.
She collapsed in the rocker
and held her head in her hands.

I visit less and less now,
afraid
(if I'm honest)
of seeing her bald head,
the bags beneath her eyes –
a disturbed kind of worry
I can't bear to witness.

She says she's having a hard day –
can't read or do the crosswords
with every blurry and bouncy letter.

I imagine her lying in bed
staring out at the rolling Wisconsin hills,
eyes dazed, fazing out reality,
becoming the infant she was so afraid
to find in my crib
years ago.

Here Is Your Map

Here is your birth: eyes blink open
to a tube of oxygen, a funny
pull and tickle at the naval.

Here is your map: a line of honey
leads you to your mother's kitchen counter
where you dab and lick.

On Clark Street, you find the blue-spotted
egg fallen from the nest
and place it in your jewelry box.

Here is your outer space: ships
that come and leave, lovers torn,
babies born. At home, you listen to her breathe.

Here is your topography: skyscrapers
bow down. Computers litter
the windowless room, typewriters click
your high-heeled song.

Your daughter thinks you're an enigma.
Marigolds bloom beneath your fingers;
the Meanies flee with just a kiss.

Your writer wants to chart this map,
tell your story;
your writer wants to eat you alive.

The Operation

I break open the chest of a beast
any beast you choose:
mastodon, elk, bald eagle.
I fish my hand through blood
and pillows of tissue.

Pulling out the arched bones,
ivory and clean as elephant tusks,
I hold them up to the sky, these
pieces of curved moon.

You lie across two rivers
joined together by prayer.
I break open your chest
and give you lungs

the power of stampedes across Africa,
flights through the Orient.
When you open your eyes
dandelion seeds fall down like tears.
I have stitched you closed with
Philodendron roots and when I say breathe
you inhale deep as the earth,
deep as a great howl in the night.

Her Hair

When I was born
she wore her dark hair
short in a pixie cut,
soft and fine.
Once the 80s hit,
her hair grew shaggy
in hairsprayed flyaways.
As I grew into
adult shoes
it turned blonde and sun-scorched
from endless gardening.
Finally, when the cancer hit,
it grew brittle and the straw pieces
fell out. I remember
finding those baby-fine strands
of silk and fragility
hugging her neck long ago.
It's *that* I mourn,
the way I fingered her hair
as a baby would,
twisting and twirling
in wonder.

The Leak

"Such is life / Falling over seven times / And getting up eight"
~JAPANESE FOLK POEM

1. He tells me she's leaking. I imagine the juice of her life drains from her brain, but it's actually from the lung where they supposedly sewed her up.

2. Before steroids, her right foot dragged. As she aims for steadiness, she glances over, nervous.

3. Upset over losing hair and eyebrows, she wears the wig with a shy finesse so I sometimes forget what lies beneath.

4. I visit on a Saturday and my stepfather plucks the cucumbers off the vine. She is also too tired to pick the tomatoes.

5. I lend her books she can focus on, ones with pictures instead of words. She's a pre-literate child.

6. I escort her up the stairs and, with a careful eye, watch her descend.

7. These are just setbacks.

8. They'll stop the leak. They'll shrink the mass. The earth does not spin in a motherless world.

The Card of No More Defeats

And am I killing you
by thinking the worst?
I feel myself dying
with drowsiness when I visit
as though under some spell.
We must seem like a Greek chorus
when we visit you –
Asking how you are with attentive
smiling faces yet behind masks
lie terrified unanswered questions.
That's why I prefer to visit you
one-on-one
when others don't tip-toe around
as if bombs hang over
the clothesline.
We sit in the kitchen sunlight
and play cards until you
exhaust yourself by trying
to match suits.
I place my hands upon yours
and beg God's healing
to wash away this death stain.
I beg this God to give us
less storms, more wars fought
then won.

If We Have a Sail

If I have magic hands, let them heal.
If I have a rifle to ward off enemies,
give me the bullets. If I have a kiss that cures,
give me your body and I will press
my lips against every sore, scrape, and mass.

If I have a voice, let me sing away this curse.
If I am a pencil, let me draw the way out.
If I am a chapel,
I open my doors to you. If I am a bed,
I spread myself down. If I have a telescope, let me
find you anywhere. If we have a sail,

let the wind carry us down-river
to a future that glows orange and iridescent
in calm water that whispers some promise
of eternity.

Homecoming

She sits cross-legged on the attic floor
before dozens of boxes of relatives' pictures,
my old playbills, baby-girl drawings.
Capped in a red handkerchief
and a bit nauseous with fever
she stares at it all.
Generations sit before her – men and women
loved and lost.
She gingerly picks up a box
as to not spill its secrets;
she doesn't want to know them yet.
That comes on the deathbed:
women whispering, spirit hands
holding hers in comfort and reassurance.
But not yet; she still has a lot of fight left.
She shakes cobwebs out of her face
and breaks open the first box.
Dust-mist rises and swirls around
her ravaged body
in recognition,
a homecoming.

The Heel

I don't know if she's ever been to New York

the kind of New York that exists
in a sort of picante mist
where sassy, hip ladies smack
cinnamon gum and walk the streets.

But my mother has worn heels.

She's driven in a fast car with a fast boy
while the mint evergreen tree sways from the mirror.

I know she's propped her leg out the window
and that just as they passed 42nd Street
her red raised heel went sailing
curved sole
tight skirt.

She could have belonged to New York:
eggrolls, newspapers flouncing down the street
with paranoid pigeons, the red stiletto
landing at the foot of a bench
in Central Park.

Now She's a Mother

Now she's a mother who needs to rest against
a pole while waiting in line.
Now she's a mother who naps every few hours,
is out of breath, who fingers
plastic straws that replace
the cigarettes that will ultimately...

Now she's a mother who must watch
me collapse like a sad accordion
and catch me open-armed,
my dying hero.

The morning dove songs annoy her,
but she still sits in her wooded palace
reading *Midwest Living* and drinking coffee.
This she did as a healthy mother,
a cancerless, massless mother.

I spend the night and Mom
cuts up strawberries for breakfast.
A glass of juice sits beside my plate
but, having forgotten, she sets down another,
scratches her head and laughs.
Now she's a mother I worry about.

Now she's a mother who takes rows
of medicine to cry less, to breathe
and think better, to help her right foot
crawl before the left.
I watch her hobble
and adjust her handkerchief
over her scarcity of hair.

Stargazing

Because in a Madeleine L'Engle book
Mom read about a "stargazing rock" –
a large rock used to lean against
while searching for stars –
we all scoured the neighborhood
for a rock mighty enough
for such a purpose
yet small enough to fit in
her little Harwood Heights
garage-side garden.

Once they moved to the
dream log home in the
country, she called me up
in near-tears and said,

      "I think I found my rock."

This was not a woman
who often had wishes granted.

I was happy.

Now she could do all
the wishing she wanted,
stargazing outside
on her acreage of land
beneath a sky
of a thousand possibilities.

One in a Thousand
on Michigan Avenue

You've gotten better, gotten worse;
you've improved or you hide it well.

You move slowly then quickly and return
to work part-time, intent on being useful.

So you speed to Chicago and stay with family,
letting my aunt see you droop the way you

can't give me flowers that will one day die.
You walk downtown with other worker bees

in business suits or high heels and in your
cute, pixie wig you resemble the mother I once knew.

You walk from train to office and strain
to forget the cancer for five or six hours

and do the frustrating work you've always
done. At this point, being one in a thousand

droning away at frustrating work is what drives
you out of bed to join this crazy world.

The Stink That Cannot Be Removed

At some point, on some day,
in my adolescent rage,
curse words spat sticky
at my mother.
Her face sheer shock:
    "Don't *ever* talk to me like that again!"
as she stormed into her bedroom
and slammed the door.

"That'll show her,"
I huffed,
puffed up by my obvious
cure for injustice.

But behind closed door
I heard her crying.
I paused in my revelry,
turning thin as Xerox.

I wanted to stay away,
hide from my stink.

But I knew I had crushed her.
Not from the R-rated slingshots,
but because she was the "who"
I threw it to.

Such words were tomahawks
hurled at her head.
She didn't have time to duck.
I didn't think to stop.

That Which Surrounds You

We are hurricanes closing in.
Our worry-dented faces and
hands fluttering in must-helps
have been called in by
the National Weather Service.
Alert the burdened cancerful woman:
best intentions can ripple so fast
that towns fall, devastated,
by love.

She Has Risen

We help you out of your chair,
a nest you have settled into with
labored breathing
and flamingo legs.
We help you rise
like a foal just getting her bearings.

Through your smile you show
discolored teeth tinted with
thirty-five years of cigarette smoke
and one year of chemotherapy.

You stand in your robe and socks,
hold our hands as we say,
"You did it!"
even though we did it…
But victories are scarce

so we let you stand tall,
my superheroine
standing eye to eye with me.

Trotter Rd. to Hwy 81

I drove away today
and swallowed hard.
I drove.
I thought:
I forgot to use your nail polish remover.
I forgot to give you that massage.
I forgot my rings on the guest dresser.
Perhaps this was on purpose
so a part of me would remain there
if only temporarily.
Maybe I left a piece of me there
since I had no idea
when I'd be back.

Suspicion

The rosebuds did not open this year
and you began to suspect.

The wind at your back
felt more like a push.

Balloons that filled the sky
like swollen swallows

saddened you because
it took such inhalation, such

exhalation. You decided to do
everything in and out, to copy

the breath and everything up
and down, to copy the chest.

But the cough, which catches you
by surprise each time,

gives you away and the head scarves
in your wardrobe tell your secrets.

PART TWO

Warship

The House of Nightmares
and of Taking Up Arms

In Rogers Park on West Pratt Street,
Gramma came to take care of me
while Mom tossed and turned in her bed –
the scene of the crime.
The nightmares and flashbacks chewed at her fingertips,
bit them flush to the skin.

Gramma sat me on her gingham lap
as Mom slept the Boogie Man away.
I sucked the grapefruit juice
from the pink, veiny half-sphere
in Gramma's palm.

At three, I repeatedly dreamt
of a shark hunting me in deep,
choking waters.
I'd run into Mom's room
and jump in her bed
as she sat up screaming.
Realizing who it was, she'd clutch me,
panting, hush me
so Gramma wouldn't hear and worry.

We'd lean against each other like book-ends;
our eyes heavy with a need
for the chase to end.
We'd both eventually sleep upright
against the headboard,
ever-ready to face
our perpetrators.

The Rape, 1981-1998

Sweetheart,

> Don't let me see you holding hands; you're not that type.
> Don't make out in the house.
> If you kiss the boys, don't let me know – just keep your
>   tongue in.
> Drink water and milk but never wine.
>
> I was raped. You could be, too.
>
> Lock your kitchen window.
> Scream all the furies into your pillow and listen to
>   Barbra Streisand records.
> Fall in love with a man twelve or thirteen years older
>   who is your own personal policeman, your own
>   Celtic knight.
>
> Drop your eyes when you stand, naked, in front of the mirror.
> Eat cheese, crackers, and a pickle for dinner every night.
> Look to the left but not the right – or to the right but not the left.
>
> Let them tear out your ovaries and hang them in your closet behind
>   your bathrobe as a reminder of the pain.
> Be your father's stranger.
> Be your mother's best friend so she is rarely your mother.
> Be her lung so without you she can't breathe.

And remember, darling,
that I love you,

Not to Surrender, but to Declare

All the mothers bring me
to the revolution,
drive me to her house where they rally
around her.

I walk through the doorway
and they say,
> Look deeper than her red handkerchief
> Deeper than her scalp

Awkward and fresh with ill-fitting news,
Mom sits in her recliner
while mothers brew coffee
and daughters, following me into
the house,
light cedarwood candles
to remind Mom of the places she's walked.
But I still smell cancer.

When first revolutions start
not many know what to do.

We drive to the mall and a daughter
tries on jeans with me.
We swap overly-expensive earrings
and I glance at Mom while she stares
ahead at nothing.
A rebellion could ignite
and she'd still sit there.

Often cancer does not comprehend
the battle.

On the ride home, a mother
and daughter play "I Spy"
in the backseat.
One calls out,
    I spy two birds singing to each other
The other answers,
    I spy one flower fighting to grow.

Sometimes cancer understands the fight.

Arriving home, a mother hands me a flag
to claim this spot as the war zone.
To wave —
not to surrender, but to declare.
Like marionettes, she positions Mom
and I facing each other.
She tells us to hug goodbye for today;
they will return tomorrow
with canons, trash cans,
and stacks of magazines.

Joining this battle takes guts
we don't yet have.

I leave, missing out on Mom's fear;
she watches me leave,
missing out on mine.

The Husbands

I think: *I am grateful that I don't*
have to live with her like you do.
I think: *I am envious that you*
get to live with her and I don't.

I wonder if there are husbands
hiding in the wine cellar
behind the bookcase,
waiting to stand beside him
when all he can do is sit.

The daughters take hold of his hands
and bring him over to me.
I stare into his sunken, defeated eyes.

He thinks: *I am grateful to be*
        the strong caretaker
He thinks: *I envy your coming*
        and going.

The Downside of Comrades

They continue to surround me.
Not just the daughters who
hold my hand
while I get ready every morning,
but now the mothers arrive.

Sometimes comradery
feels like a swarm.

Dozens sit around my apartment
and their daughters lounge with them.
Some sit in an embrace, others
chat with arms linked together.
Bottles bob in pots on my stove.
Even babies coo their presence.

Sometimes I watch the mothers
touch their daughters' hands
and cheeks. They touch
each other's realities.

Other times I smell
the stinking cancer, stomp out
of my bedroom and yell,
> But you breathe so easy!
> You aren't going anywhere!

The Turning

When I speak of the turning,
I speak of ships coming in
at high tide.
Mothers pack first aid kits
and minestrone soup.
Daughters pull in rowboats of magazines
not to be read but browsed.
Husbands below deck roll
cigars they know will comfort
the would-be widow
if only smoke wasn't outlawed
in the house.
So they bring out
The American Journal of Police
to keep him interested, instead.

When I speak of the turning
I mean the new smell
invading the house:
a sickening sweet
mixed with rot.
I hated to visit her then.
I didn't want directions to change
nor any progress made
on the now-straight path
to the inevitable.

Prisoner of War

You have come for her on the battlefield
but I stand in the way.
You've tied her to the pole
with IV tubes.
She feels faint, weak,
and can't make me out
through the smoke and debris.

Promise me she will awaken.
Promise that all that's at stake
is one of two lungs
and not her life.

Take me, instead.
Tie my throat closed. I'll keep focused
on her face.
I don't have anyone
who needs me so much.

Take me, instead.
No one will know.

Attic Illness

It went from living room
to attic
and as you stumbled, lopsided,
you asked
    What gnaws on my brain?

I didn't know who you'd be
with one missing lung
and brain under attack.
I couldn't bear to watch
so I turned away.

Cars passed with families eating newly-
picked apples. Sweet dribbled down
their chins. Along the road, sunflowers grew
shy and tall despite the drought.

I couldn't stand the joy.
Sometimes a soldier in the trenches
needs to bury her head in the sand.

It went from living room
to attic,
this diseased enemy.
I vowed to fight it
so in fatigues
with rifle and flashlight
I climbed the steps
and fired.

I'll Meet You in Her Closet

For Alison Townsend

We stand parallel,
our mothers both sick.
You're a nine-year-old with two ropes
of braided hair down your back,
caught in the grip of the 1960s.

I'm hating who I've become now,
stuck at different speed bumps
along the way.
I'm twenty-eight and hate who I am
yet seek forgiveness from a Source
I don't yet know.

In 1962 and 2006, our mothers
hinge on death.
In your blue book
with the gorgeously-gowned woman
on the cover, I recognize a fellow soldier
fighting for the revolution.

But unlike a brave recruit, I want to
hide in your mother's closet
under her fur coat and run my fingers
through the waves of your
little-girl-loosened hair.

You look heavenward and pray
on scabby knees.
To me, it's a dark ceiling and I look
into your mournful eyes and say,
    "My mother will not die."

I shrink to nine, your equal,
and we hold onto each other
as land mines go off all around,
setting off the closet's
mothball scent.

Butterfly

Black butterflies nest
in your left lung,
exiles from the right.
You lean against me
as the sun sighs down
and I sing every lullaby I know.

We sit amidst a war
and I don't know who's winning.

I feel you sleep-heavy with the kind
of quiet you never found
when I was young.
I hold you close though
I smell gunsmoke.

The tenebrous clouds roll in;
I'm frightened
of their opacity.
I squeeze your bony shoulder;
your hand flutters
as you cough.

PART FOUR

Griefship

Floweret

It is not by accident
that we keep
rotting flowers.

We love the dying.
Separating the rose
to dissect its beauty

we find the beginning.
What was once a velvet
bulb with back-bending

stomachs is now seed.
We play with eternal sleep,
wanting to drive into that realm

then home to tell
our colleagues
that flowers are,

indeed, living
on the other side.
Why do we give them

to our little prom girls,
so new and glistening,
to take them home

and dry them upside-
down, a hangman
already in life?

Keep the Road to Somewhere Lit

When I got off the phone with my stepfather, his voice
hoarse and scared, when I let the fact of my mother's death
settle on the first filmy layer of my brain, I instinctively lit
all the candles in the room.

Before the tears, before the full realization of a lost
appendage, my room flickered with the glow of a chapel.

Did I grasp the light to the land of the living?
Where was it that she went?
As tears began to show up like rushed party guests,
I cried, *Mom, Mommy, just don't forget me in the dark.*

Let This Be Our Secret

Last Monday
the blood clot ended
the year-long fight
against your body.

Your husband tried
and tried to resurrect you
with breathy kisses
and failed.

Don't tell anyone,
but I've spotted you since
and they aren't just in dreams.
I see you at the mall

now that holiday shoppers
are on the rise.
I sense you watching
outside my bedroom window

while I cry
and I know you want in
as much as I want out.
So if you open my window

I won't tell.
No one has to know.

Smoke

It's what finally did you in,
even after it all left your lungs
in a collection of marching ghost soldiers
or so we thought –
Your lungs did not leave *it*.
Water could not extinguish it completely.

Fire raged inside you as you sat
each morning with a cigarette
between your fingers, coupled with coffee
the color of a cat's eye.

The leveling of your chest sucked you in
over the years. You'd cough and wake up the child
in a bundle of worry.
Then, this past January, the diagnosis appeared
and you began to chew on straws
instead of tobacco sticks.

The deaths came on as if by permission.
They took the lung out and your body
collapsed further into itself. How could
empty space hold court in your chest?
I patted your right side gently,
afraid you would implode.

You stopped the want that stretched
from pubescence to middle-age; do you know?
Now that you're gone, your husband
has reclaimed the habit?

The death halos are back, polluting your house.
After exhaling, he reaches out as though
it has formed your frame, but it dissipates.
He cries tears that roll down
his neck and they, too, evaporate.

Endangered Species

The radio announcer said
the whooping cranes are now in Tennessee.

They're following a small airplane

across the country: Operation Mirgration.
How easily their abandoned hearts
must have turned toward the steel bird,

looking for a mother, mentor, guide.
Much in the same way, I flip through
my address book in search of women

whose arms wrap around, whose bosoms
are big and still lactate.
The whooping cranes

are North America's most
endangered bird. They all follow me

through the azure sky as I soar above
towns and cities.
They follow me in hopes that

one day I'll be able to care for them.
My fear is that we shall all
become endangered together.

That we'd fly through a cloud and
    – poof –
not come out the other side.

The Grief of the Husband

Wielding a nightly scotch in hand,
you didn't know you got too close.
It was the day your wife died
and I, your stepdaughter,
was the only female part of her left.

It was not your fault you got too
close to me. You were sleep-deprived,
booze-bamboozled;
all you saw were her hands as mine,
that same hazel speck in my eyes.

You did nothing wrong but lose
your candor a bit, put your nose
to mine and say,
      "You're *my* daughter now,"

and even though I shook in my shoes,
turned into a scared, single-digit age,
I nodded. Your eyes were crazed,
corneas shook, tears welled up, breath stank
and settled over my face like a scrim.

      "I'll take care of you," you said, "Now hug me."
I did so tentatively until you shouted,
      "With two arms!"
and so I wrapped both around you
like a prickly tree Mom once said I could trust
and I felt the blood inside me clot.

You squeezed and squeezed
wishing she'd
burst from me like a genie
out of a bottle.

Commodity

I've been writing about you forever.

> Elegies, obituaries, sharing secrets
> you'd bribe me not to tell.
> Some, maybe, you'd let spill.

It is possible to be sick of you.
> I love you too much and
> I'm beginning to loathe your ghost
> that directs my pen this way
> and that.

Put a pretty hat on my bald head, you say
> and I reply, "No, truth is more quaking and hits harder."

And you ask, *My sweet, heartbroken girl, are you going*
> *to sell me out?*

"Death, is it not true /
you are everyone's lover…"
~ JUDE NUTTER, *"Crow"*

I have sought you out since youth;
I've sat in rows of library books telling your
tales of conquering the world
as you slowly incinerated me.
Your lies tasted sweet and the juice
dripped down my chin and plopped
onto the pages of the DSM.

Poets write about you as an ending,
the antithesis to life, but you and I
have a sordid past.
You crooned your swan song to me
and I fell head over heels
down the cobwebbed stairs
to the bottom where you kept
me captive,
addicted to wounds.

Older and more mature now,
I see you as neither romantic nor pleasant,
with your dead morning breath, long arms,
spindly legs.
You are simply the reality-kick to those
who think life deserves to be thrown away
with the clumpy cat litter.

You have dominion if we so choose
but, if not, if you are but a blink,
a cough that fades,
you still manage to whisper,
  Open your eyes, lover, to this crazy world.
  Do not think you're the only one.

The Difference in Multiplication

The mother is 37

Her daughter's brown pigtails wave
when she laughs

She practices for a math test

Mother points out a fact as the girl
leans against her sweatered shoulder

For a study break, the girl skips
across the front lawn

Back at the table, the girl dreams of
high school and what college will bring

The girl learns multiplication; life
times life equals more

She decides after four boyfriends
she'll pick a husband

The mother chuckles sweet and
curls in around her girl

The daughter goes through every
flashcard with precision

The mother is 52

The daughter twirls the straight, dark
hair around her finger as she once did

They go over the mother's will

The mother hiccups tears and puts
her head in her hands

Both feel sunk, caught subterranean

The daughter turns pages of an
oncology unit pamphlet

They quickly learn subtraction and
the daughter can't bear the negative

She knows her mother will widow the
man she loves

Daughter sighs heavy and holds up
her crying mother

The mother signs the will;
daughter helps navigate the pen

Pacifier

After Maxine Kumin's "The Sunday Phone Call"

It's 8:00 in the morning -
the hour I'd call her
to start my day.

If we had time now to talk,
she'd list the food I need
to fill my empty fridge.

You need to clean once in a while, too.

"But I'm tired, Ma. I miss you."

Don't use me as an excuse to slip away.

This I'd ignore and continue bemoaning,
"My tears add up every night and flood this place."

Don't doom yourself. Your cat needs you. And you must make
chocolate éclairs for your one-day daughter.

"My daughter?" I'd scoff. "I'm as lonely as a meow in the
snow. I have no lover, mother; I have no one and I'm
nearing thirty."

She'd laugh at my naïveté and I'd stomp:
"No! Because of you I'm stuck at age twenty-eight,
forever November 6, 2006. I'm blind and deaf
and I am stuck."

And she'd sigh, *"My Lisa, please stop talking and listen to me."*

And because her requests are meaningful, I would.

"But you're not saying anything."

Exactly, she'd smile through the phone. *Just listen to me breathe.*

So I'd lean against the wall
with the phone to my ear
like a pacifier to the mouth
and listen
for a very long time.

June Night

If you think I have stopped grieving
ask the oceans I have created.
Ask the women in the rowboat
just grateful to be alive
after the tsunami.

I bear few scars
from my years of self-injury,
but I scrape and scar
while I climb inside my cave-
wound and hibernate with
a corpse.

Quinces

"She had died in the first week of quinces"
~ BRENDA HILLMAN, *"Secret Knowledge"*

A magazine told me that
quinces are for poets.
If you cut and boil them
the ugly fur-covered fruit would
turn to sweet honey goodness.

I never had time to cook quinces for her.

I wanted to show I could stir
up some magic,
take care of myself.
Surely, time over the stove
with that thick, sweet aroma
would propel me into adulthood.

What a shame;
we never had time to grow
nor time to collect
the harvest.

One Year in the River Lethe

A year can congeal a brain —
      anaesthetize, get chilblains.

Mama, I'm cold.

There goes the ferry of memory —
    no way of holding on.
Wearisome water separates us.

Mama, I'm cold.

This year has been scrambled,
      dislocated, found only in a life
I haven't led. I am not the woman
I thought I'd wax into.

Mama, I'm cold.

It's forever Fall, portending a miscarriage
      of life, freezing the embryo so it always
burns for mothering.
Mama, I'm wintry in this loosened womb; Mama,

    I'm cold.

52

I'm sure this is not the last
poem I will write,
not the last time I conjure you up
out of ashes to a petite woman
in knit sweaters and hip huggers.

When I think of you it is not in
head scarves or with under-eye bags,
but in a business suit and high heels.
I think of you in a summertime smock
with dirt beneath fingernails,
basket of cucumbers at your side.

I'm sure this is not your last poem
because I hold you under my tongue
like a lozenge that soothes a sore throat.

But as long as I recall the clicking of heels
as I rouse from sleep, you are still
alive. As long as cucumbers want to be picked,
you continue to beat through me
waiting for me to claim my life.

May I Be Excused?

Dear Mom, I hope you don't mind
me calling other mothers, looking for
other arms, other storm cellars,
red painted fingernails, whispers of sleep,
other beds in which to rest, cheeks to kiss,
hands to examine.

Dear Mom, I hope you don't mind me
asking the nightmares to stop,
the memories to soften, become easier
to swallow. I hope you don't mind
if I take a different step,
then a different one and then
different again, so then, Mom,

can you see me dancing?

Anniversary in Autumn

Autumn arrives and it knows
more than I do.
Leaves line the gutters like gold coins.
I drive beneath red-headed trees
and remember last year

when I drove past these Autumn streaks
to her house. She sat,
nesting in her easy chair,
one lung fading into her eventual end.
Fall knows it owns
my going-down.

That year, I painted her nails
poppy-red – anything to add color.
Her husband put out garlands
of leaves, woolen scarecrows,
and fiber optic pumpkins.
Each in the wrong place, but she
didn't mind.

We lost her as the cold set in.
He left the fall décor up for months,
not wanting to disturb the silence
she had left.
And now I see trees fail to hold on;
leaves turn barren again.

It's true this world spins in seasons.
This year, the leaves spit out from my wheels
as I drive aimlessly,
picturing her in the easy chair,
head drooping
like a sunflower
past its prime.

Spell of Motherly Resurrection

Dip a pocket watch and a sparrow's feather
into a bowl of saliva collected from her sleep
long ago when she was alive.

Kiss a sealed envelope with her name scribbled on it
and distill that into the mixture.

Stare at her picture until three tears take the plunge.

At this point you have a time machine.

> Travel back to your fifteenth year
> and let her in your locked door; let her help you
> through the fear and trembling.

> At twenty-one, after she compares you
> to her much-missed mother,
> liken your hands to hers
> to create a dotted line.

> At twenty-eight, November 6th,
> stand where she collapses in the bathroom.
> Be there and, by God, let her go the way of all flesh.

Stir her pooled-purple sweater into the pot.
Let her scent of Prell and cigarettes
rise to the ceiling.
Next, hold the pot up to the sky.
A sparrow will fly down and take
the handles.

> And that's all you'll get, I'm sorry.
Didn't you know an orphan kind of loss
carries no remedy?

But you look at the calendar on the wall:
> It is November 7th, one day after
her head scarves scattered, one day toward
learning of a world with no such illusion.

PART FIVE

Stepship

The Heaviest Confession

"my mother, alas, alas,
did not always love her life,
heavier than iron it was
[...]But the iron thing they carried, I will not carry."
  ~ MARY OLIVER, *"Flare"*

She wants me to tell you she wasn't perfect.
To write about shushing her drunken boyfriend

outside our house at midnight.
I did hear them. I could pick out her voice from wind,

laughter, from birds collected for company.
Her song played the loudest, the longest.

"But tell them of the scotch," she sighs and so I tell you
of the amber liquid rippling over the rocky, icy surface,

the drink I knew was for relief at the end of every day while
she read her latest Oprah's Book Club selection.

All I know is that my days don't end with a glass of scotch and I am
the one in our family to put an end to escapism, much later

than anticipated, but I still owe her that due.
She wants me to tell you she wasn't perfect, that sometimes

her song was warbled from crying, from the weight of it all.
She wants me to tell you that she died a little bit lost

and wants more for the rest of us down here.

Memory in Origami

for Lee

Someday, I will remember
what I learned to forget:

Her morning coffee cup sitting
in a slant of light, her head asleep
on her pillow, lips slightly parted,
    breathing,
        breathing,
            breathing.

How can a day pass without her
when I now have so much?

He loves me and lets me hide
in his arms, fold myself
into an origami woman.

He holds me when I hiccup with sobs,
when my teary eyes
tremble oceanic earthquakes.

    He helps me remember
what I learned to forget:

How she told me I'd dance with a man
in the kitchen
and that meant true love
and would stick.

I'd not lose it like a sock in the dryer;
it wouldn't threaten me with harm
like a hornet dancing crazy-eights
near my face.

Perhaps leaves fall in autumn
to cover the grieving.
He brushes the foliage off me,
unfolds and welcomes me
to walk on these paper-thin legs.

His arms re-imagine me into a wife,
part of a family that will keep.

Island

for the boy, mid-2008

This is a strange land. I meet
my future
      stepson first.
A one-and-a-half-year-old whose cries
fill the room. With touring hands,
he searches for trouble in everything:
      box, tablecloth, shoe.
He places hand upon Daddy's shoulder,
stares at me.

The two girls join my
new charge and I am
more than a babysitter who must
have six eyes;
      I am Daddy's girlfriend.

But it's just us now, with Daddy at work.
We're on an island, a forced
get-to-know-you.
The trees are play-doh,
the sand made of whispers.
They want to run to the deep end

but I place my tender hooks
in them to keep the sharks away.
They're not sure what to make
of me; they use me like a utensil
only good for meals and yet

there are times when,
in their sleep,
one rolls over and presses
her hand in mine,

as if to make sure
I'll still be there
in the morning.

I suddenly know
I could come in great use
        to their fragile, little hearts.

10 and 5

for the girls, Christmas 2008

I am not a mother yet.
I've lost a mother, but I'm not a mother,
except to myself on days I hold my waist
and rock, tending to the weak.

But tomorrow, you (10) and you (5)
will come to visit your father
and meet "the girlfriend."

At first you'll dismiss me
like a fish swimming beneath
the ice you stand upon
but what you don't know is one day
I'll be your stepmother,
the Mama bear who tucks you in
every other week and then,
after time, every single night.

I will be there for breakfasts and dinners.
I will want to hear about your day.

Will you (10) let me into your scalded heart?
Will you (5) stop kicking and spitting your pain
enough to see my lap as warm and safe?

Will either of you be still enough
for me to kiss your head?

And when you (10 and 5) go home, your Daddy
and I will smile and I will no longer need to rock myself.

I wish I could call my mother up and tell her:
"Not in a sonogram, but I just saw my future!
They walked right through my front door."

She'd nod, smile, and say
she'd been watching all along.

He and I will watch our kids bound away in the grass
until one year later when
I am official, a woman who loves you,
mother-like but kept apart
a few steps away.

Struck by Lightning, Laughing

Is this a cosmic joke?
That I marry into
a family with three children?

For three years I've stumbled through
parenting without kitchen table advice
without her phone number
to call late at night
when my head is sore from
hair-pulling.

Is this a joke that I'm propelled
into motherhood
three years after losing my own?

Someone somewhere must have faith
I can do this.
An assignment of this kind
is not random.

Motherless mothers mumble,
        "Not fair"
but our hearts bleed open
for our children.

I search through her albums for advice,
her recipe books in search
of a cure for teenage rebellion
and childhood whine.

I come to realize that I've been placed here
specifically, tenderly,
and that the most random things
take faith.

For I love my little
chaos machines
in a way I never could have fathomed,
the way I know Mom loved
her own crazy hurricane.

Not this Womb, but this Heart

Once upon a time there was
a good stepmother who banished
all the evil ones away.
Generations of stepmothers grew full bellies
upon the arrival of other women's children.

See my belly? It's as if you are in there
and the first *I love you* will burst me open
and tears will flow out of me
because I love you so much, worry so much,
want you so to be mine.

July 4, 2009

For G who has since come a long way

I've been told you are
as dangerous as fireworks.
Your fury doesn't know where to go
so, like a firecracker, you explode out
the top of your head – sparks fly,
the sound barrier threatened.

Sweet girl, at your other house
you torment your sister
and I think it's because you
yearn for her love the most.

I know something about pushing away
those we love the deepest, but I saw
how you swam with her in the lake –
as though she was your North Star.

One July 4th I drove from Sauk City
to Madison and saw fireworks
illuminate the sky
from neighboring towns.

I thought of my mother, years gone,
and how I exploded in my teen years,
slicing knife into forearm
when, really, I just wanted to know
she loved me despite my faults.

This 4th of July
I cry as colored sparks reflect
off my windshield.
Sad that you feel you have to
threaten
to get her love,
sad that you hate so much
and get no reassurance.

If You Knew it is I Who Sing

For A, who rebels in 2012

If you knew, in your rage, fury
and emotional claustrophobia,
that the one you can't stand
to think of as a "parent"
walked in your steps
and exploded angst on her body
just as you do now...
If you knew, what would you do?

It's me —
the one you call goody-goody,
who sings while washing dishes,
who cries at movies
or a touching gift.
I must seem so soft to you
and yet so hard
like when my eyebrows arch in disappointment
after finding the condom
or when my tongue spits daggers, reminding
you when you're late
for school.
You hate this, of course:
my parental darts.

Perhaps hypocrite, perhaps wuss,
I don't know how you
view me.
Certainly not "cool" as you once did.
No more singing "The Little Mermaid" for you
and seeing your wide-eyed wonderment.
My novelty has flown south
with the birds of childhood.

Now I am a permanent fixture,
another parent to guide and watch you,
you who were not watched long ago
when you needed watching.

If you knew
that I, too, was not watched
and hid in my bedroom-cave,

if somehow my 14-year-old self
could hang out with you
for a day,
would we ignite
from the pain sparked between us?

But if somehow
at age 24 —
old enough to have learned
yet too young to preach —
I could visit you,
would you let me in?

Because I am 34 today
and all your doors are closed;
friends understand more
and parents are the worst preachers.

If you knew
that I am no enemy,
if you knew
that I sometimes scream inside
instead of sing,
what, then?

I wish I could reach you
and have you hear me.
Until then, I will be a witness
to your testimony
and keep singing
our redemptive future.

The Mother Who Wasn't

Childless, I hold countless
children inside. This month I bleed
an extra blood-letting due to confused
hormones and wonder
if I lose them in each clot,
but they remain hushed
like chanting nuns

Red makes me feel the most blue.

I remember Mom telling me at twelve
that I bleed to bear babies and I imagined
baby after baby slipping from my uterus
as I fainted on a starch-white bed.

Now, with husband and stepchildren,
I am busy with
dishes, homework, the occasional cough syrup,
and bedtime books.

Afterward, I lie still in bed. The moon's pull
tugs at me through the east window.
It wants babies and calls for the ocean's
current to rock me toward birth,
but the blood continues
to break against the tides
each month.

I cannot give birth to my stepchildren
and make them mine. Though I learn to love,
delight, and eventually, sacrifice,
I still hear my parallel universe:

babies crying
their vowels to me,
babies listening to their heartsick mother
call out their unused names.

What the Stepmother Gives

for Mom and Lyn, in love and appreciation

Mothers pass down hair color
and shyness. They teach
suckling and bonding.
Womb to tomb, her embrace
etches around her child's body.

I love my mother.

The stepmother cleans up messes
made by now-defunct families;
the parents the child longs for
are a faraway fairy tale.
The stepmother accepts
second-place in the children's eyes
      and she loves them anyway.

I love my stepmother.
And now that I am one, I see:
      not all stories are the same.

The stepmother may have to
attempt to be a grade A mama
while in the shadow
      of trying not-to-be.
The child will pin the blue ribbon
on the mom even if
the stepmother helps with all
the homework, notices a change
in clothing size,
      hugs the raw heartache.

The only thank-you
is ten or twenty years away.
The stepmother keeps an eye

on the horizon.

Stepmothers pass down
the ability to bend,
adjust, adapt.
She stretches a child's heart
to include one who might not
　　　have birthed her
　　　or handed down a beauty mark
on the tiny bottom;

she is the last piece
in a disjointed jigsaw puzzle.

The Covenant that Saved Me

for my Savior, 2010 and always

I am not a wild child,
but when my mother died
I made a pact with something dark —

that I would do anything
to distract myself from
the aching, bruised grief.

I let anyone into my home who would
understand I wanted comfort —
sometimes furious, sometimes tender.

I told myself
this was okay.

But the next night I'd only be sobbing
and lonely again as grief would peck
at my face until it bled and quickly, so quickly,
life escalated down to depths of hell
I'd never known.

I can only say I'm sorry, Lord, for giving up my
rawest places to those who knew nothing of me,
and I'm sorry to who I am now

who had no idea that, two years later,
I'd meet the man who should get all those things:
love, grief, my body.

I'm sorry, Lord, for turning to others
instead of You. Though I don't deserve it,
You love and comfort me better than anyone else.

The pact is past now, but regrets

haunt me. Please,
can You go back and tell me I'll meet
my husband so soon after
all those mistakes?
That I will become a mother of three
instantaneously

and that my mother in Heaven would stand up
in ovation after ovation?

Can you go back to that darkened pact, God,
and erase it?

      No,
because the things a storm can bring
are wondrous. Your Son walked on the sea
and beckoned His friend outside his comfort.

I know You call me forth.
I know You forgave me before I ever asked
and now that I am Yours, my life is blessed
with after-tsunami blooms.

I am grateful as only those who have
survived pacts such as these
can be.
I am grateful for the twenty-eight years
I had with my mother,

The Sheila Rae Brodsky who rests with You now
and I am grateful to call You my Father
after years of seeking truth,

comfort, and a love unfailing.
You saved me, Lord. My pact,
my covenant is with You.

Moon as Surrogate

Now I look into the face of the moon and see the kind
womanly features you talked about.

I dreamed, after your death, that you took care of me.
I dreamed, after my death, that I took care
of these children.

Resurrection helped my parenting skills.

At first, stepmotherhood was like a honeymoon:
drenched in love, awe, and comfy blankets.
I ran after them to tickle, kiss, tuck in,

but Mom –
you didn't tell me of women who go mad.

By predisposition, by chemical imbalance,
by phase or season, I don't know – there are times
I pick at my wounds, paralyze time
and times I band-aid up the pain and swear
I can't do this anymore.

When the moon waxes, I seem to love
them more and my womb expands
to embrace the whole universe. But when it wanes,
I close up, tolerate less, spit needles
and just want quiet,
an island.

Can one love with these variables?

But I remember the woman you told me
lived in the moon and how she followed me closely
throughout every tide, wax, and wane.

I know now of the God who exists above everything,
who rounded the moon with His hands, who
blew the leaves across my path to startle me
the other way.

Who gave life
took life away
and continues to give and take again.

I imagine this God
forgiving my wolf-howling fluctuations.

I trust God sees my horizon
when I can't,
and I trust He'll breathe for me
should my own lungs
one day
like impermanent butterfly wings
fold closed.

Born and raised in Chicago, IL, LISA MARIE BRODSKY was the Martha Meir Renk Graduate Fellow at the University of Wisconsin-Madison where she received an M.F.A. in Poetry in 2005. She has been featured on Madison Public Radio, WISC-TV, and in *Madison Magazine*. Her poetry, fiction, and creative non-fiction have been published in *The North American Review* (as a finalist for the James Hearst Poetry Prize), *Circle Magazine*, *The Southern Ocean Review*, *Hippocampus Magazine*, *VerseWisconsin*, *Pirene's Fountain*, among others. She is the Wisconsin Director for the Alzheimer's Poetry Project and writes about the illness in her poetry chapbook, "We Nod Our Dark Heads" (Parallel Press, 2008). Brodsky works in Madison, WI as a vocational assistant for adults with disabilities and lives in Evansville, WI, with her husband and three stepchildren.